Nawaz Sharif
Fahd Shah
Mahir Rehman

ROLE OF TEACHERS IN CAREER COUNSELLING AT SECONDARY SCHOOL LEVEL

Nawaz Sharif
Fahd Shah
Mahir Rehman

ROLE OF TEACHERS IN CAREER COUNSELLING AT SECONDARY SCHOOL LEVEL

Career, Counselling, School, Teacher

Noor Publishing

Imprint
Any brand names and product names mentioned in this book are subject to trademark, brand or patent protection and are trademarks or registered trademarks of their respective holders. The use of brand names, product names, common names, trade names, product descriptions etc. even without a particular marking in this work is in no way to be construed to mean that such names may be regarded as unrestricted in respect of trademark and brand protection legislation and could thus be used by anyone.

Cover image: www.ingimage.com

Publisher:
Noor Publishing
is a trademark of
Dodo Books Indian Ocean Ltd. and OmniScriptum S.R.L publishing group

120 High Road, East Finchley, London, N2 9ED, United Kingdom
Str. Armeneasca 28/1, office 1, Chisinau MD-2012, Republic of Moldova, Europe
Printed at: see last page
ISBN: 978-620-7-47909-2

Dedicated

To

My Parents and my Respected Teachers

ROLE OF TEACHERS IN CAREER COUNSELLING

AT SECONDARY SCHOOL LEVEL

Table of Contents

CHAPTER 1

INTRODUCTION

1.Background of the Study

Secondary school education plays important role in the development of student (National Education Policy, 2009). It is a stage in which students choose subjects that will contribute to potential careers. Secondary schools with appropriate career advice allow students to have successful future careers and prosperous life (WATSON, 2009). Secondary school students face a real challenge in making acceptable career choices and subject selections based on interest and aptitude (Issa&Nwalo) 2008). The majority of high school graduates do not receive good career advice, which leads to low results and trouble obtaining desired occupations or careers (Maree, 2009).

Teachers play a critical role in offering career advice to students (Khan, 2011). Teachers assist students in choosing school subjects appropriate for their abilities and will allow them to have successful careers in the future (Flayer& Adams, 2008). According to Garrahy (2001), teachers are the primary providers of career advice, assisting students in subject selection and providing career knowledge. Students with little to no career encouragement from teachers at the secondary school level, according to Maree and Beck (2004), are unlikely to achieve their desired future careers. According to Elizabeth (2012), teachers play a role in secondary school students' career decisions by providing information and advising them about obtaining such jobs. Teachers assess students' skills, inform them about the subjects they are studying, and teach them how to move forward with their chosen professions (Kisilu Kimani & Combo, 2012).

According to Foskett et al. (2008), teachers are important agents in secondary school students' career decisions. They say that teachers shape students' attitudes and responses in preparation for their future careers. According to Mudhovozi and Chireshe (2012), teachers greatly impact students' career decisions because they provide them with career knowledge and assistance in subject selection. Kniveton (2004) discovered that secondary school teachers serve as role models and facilitators for students, guiding them in a subject selection based on their strengths and expectations. Secondary school teachers influence students' attitudes toward specific professions and students typically pursue those career paths (Denga, 2004).

In secondary schools, teachers serve as guides. They inform students about possible professions and the entry criteria and job results they can expect if they choose those careers (Dondo, 2006). Teachers have a huge impact on students' job goals and final career choices. Teachers provide career counselling, career statistics, topic selection, and career outcomes (Shumba&Naong, 2012). Khan, Murtaza, and Shifa (2012) have claimed that teachers play a significant role in secondary school students' career choices. Their influence is even more visible in school subject selection and career detail. As a result, secondary school teachers serve as role models for students deciding on a career path.

Teachers were identified as resource persons by Metheny et al. (2008) to provide vocational guidance to students. Secondary school teachers, consciously or unknowingly, affect their students' future career paths. According to Swift (2009), teachers know their students and choose subjects based on their interests. According to Goard (2000), teachers are extremely beneficial to secondary school students because they teach them what they can become in the future. Teachers in Pakistani schools offer informal career advice to secondary school students and assist them in choosing suitable occupations, according to Kiani (2010).

Teachers are critical in supporting students' career guidance, according to Howard et al. (2009).

1.1 Statement of the Problem

It can be assumed that teachers in secondary school level play an important role in providing career identifying their career preferences and aptitudes, and finding possible careers. The researchers investigated the role of teachers in secondary school career guidance, who were interested in the importance of teachers in secondary school career guidance.

1.2 Objectives of the Study

1. The research shall precisely attempt to achieve the following objectives:
2. To identify the major concern of career counselling with the student's futures
3. To analysis the impacts of career counselling on student's performance
4. To know the importance of career counselling at Secondary school level in Islamabad.

Delimitations of the Study

The delimitations of the study were to:

1. Secondary school level.
2. Secondary school students.
3. Islamabad

Significance of the Study

The significance of this study is to explore, analyse the impacts of the career counselling factors accordingly and try to promote positive impacts of career counselling on student's educational performance at Secondary school level, prevailing a comfortable environmental benefiting students for the representation of themselves at any stages throughout the world. And also tried to conduct seminars on display screen to spread awareness about career counselling in Islamabad

Operational Definitions

Carer

Career is a series of connected employment opportunities, where you build up skills at jobs over time.it often considered to be the pursuit of a life long

Counselling

counseling is a professional service that involves helping individuals couples, families or group address and manage various personal and social and psychological challenges the goals of counselling is to support client in understanding and resolving these issues improving their mental health and wellbeing and facilities personal growth .

Career counselling

Career counseling focused on helping individual understanding and navigates their career clients in making informed decisions about their careers and achieving professional fulfilment. Key element of career counselling includes.

CHAPTER NO .2

LITERATURE REVIEW

2. Career counselling theories

Nora G (2008), clarified various speculations on profession counselling as they can be sketched out beneath: Coordinating Theories (Trait/factor): Based on differential brain science, these methodologies accept that counseling is basically about a procedure of reasonable basic leadership where customers are surveyed by the „expert practitioner" and afterward coordinated to the „best fit" opportunity. It pursues that the arrangement of data about the 24 customer and the universe of work will bring about conduct change (for example improved basic leadership abilities).

This hypothesis has been created by Parson in 1908. Developmental hypothesis: The way toward helping an individual to create and acknowledge an incorporated and sufficient picture of himself and of his job in the realm of work. A focal idea is that individuals create through stages over their lifetime. This hypothesis has been started Ginsberg et al. (1951) who proposed three life stages which extensively compared with ordered age, and Donald Super who was a doctoral student of Ginsberg's and created a large number of Ginsberg's thoughts.

Hypothesis of word related portion (opportunity structure): Apart from a favored minority of the populace people are (pretty much) compelled in their selection of occupations by social factors that are beyond their ability to do anything about for example sex, ethnicity and social class. This hypothesis was first proposed by Roberts (1968) as an option in contrast to hypotheses of career improvement progressed by Ginsberg and Super. Learning hypothesis of careers decision and advising: People get their inclinations through an assortment of learning encounters; convictions about themselves and the idea of their reality rise through immediate and circuitous instruction encounters. They make a move based on their convictions utilizing learned abilities. The first hypothesis (Krumholtz et al, 1976, Mitchell and Krumholtz, 1990) is otherwise called the social learning hypothesis of profession basic leadership Psychodynamic speculations: (Krumholtz et al, 1976, Mitchell and Krumholtz, 1990)

These hypotheses guided by endeavors to comprehend, make significance of, and use singular thought processes, purposes and drives to help career advancement.

Anne Roe (1956) is the originator of this hypothesis. Network connection hypothesis: According to this hypothesis, the most noteworthy factors in word related decision are the relational exchanges led in neighborhood settings. The hypothesis has been started by Law in 1981. The laid out above hypothesis have been examined by Nora Gikopoulou (2008) and our exploration will be much worried by yet not constrained to the Learning hypothesis of careers decision and counselling. In this examination, distinctive process is done to research variables influencing college student's execution.

The focal point of this examination is that student execution in middle assessment is connected with students" framework comprised of his methodology towards correspondence, learning offices, appropriate counselling and family worry in this examination I have inferred that there is a positive connection between Communication, learning offices, legitimate counselling and student execution. There is additionally a negative connection between family stress and students" execution. In this way, in this exploration, I turned out with an end underscoring that legitimate counselling has an impact on students" execution. (Lazarus and Chinwe, 2011) completed an investigation on the job of Guidance Counsellor on Career Improvement and their discoveries were that Guidance advisors work independently and with different teachers to meet the formative needs everything being equal, incorporating those with unique needs or incapacities.

v Fundamentally, they centre on the scholarly, career, and individual/social formative needs all things considered, including those with extraordinary needs.

Irregularities in the jobs of rehearsing counselling advisors have caused a few experts in instruction to start to address the developing job of the advisor in regards to student with unique needs, particularly concerning their profession improvement. Since the degree of bliss an individual oozes in life is firmly identified with the sort of career the individual picks, and other profession advancement exercises identifying with work maintenance and progression, counselling guides must undertaking to open their student's to a few career improvement exercises so as to push them to effectively, pick occupations, get ready for, go into and progress in them In the investigation embraced by (Ali, 2014), it was discovered that the degree of counselling and advising administrations among the student's in the college was not essentially high.

There was critical impact in scholastic execution of student who had gotten counselling and guiding administrations as against the individuals who had not. (Lazarus and Chinwe 2011) completed an examination on the components influencing student's execution and discovered that Students" learning inclinations, class participation, passage capabilities and requirements, the impact of age furthermore, sexual orientation are significant determinants of scholarly execution In his exploration entitled "Career Guidance in Rwanda Higher Education. A basic investigation", (Irafasha) 2010) turned out with the discoveries expressing that Some of the issues in Rwanda identified with profession counselling incorporate various implications of profession counselling, deficiently created coordination of institutional exercises, fixed status of career focuses in advanced education organizations and absence of methodical logical inquire about in connection to career advancement.

For the most part, in this writing, it very well may be seen that there are a few elements affecting the students" scholastic execution, for example, correspondence, learning offices, legitimate counselling, family stress, class size, Statistic factors, inspiration Students" learning inclinations, class participation, section capabilities and essentials. Despite the fact that

Counselling is among these elements, a couple of explores have been led on its job upon the students" a few researches have been conducted on its role upon the student's performance and there is need of conducting more researches on career Counselling (Irafasha , 2010)

Current problems in school-based career guidance and education

School leavers today are facing a more difficult situation than ever, because rapid advances in technology have meant that knowledge and skills traditionally taught in school may not relate adequately to the job opportunities of the immediate future (Hirschi, 2018; Perry et al., 2010; Skorikov, 2007; To achieve this goal, policy-makers worldwide will need to prioritize career guidance practices in schools and explore how teachers can better prepare their students for the future (OECD, 2004, 2011, 2018).

It has become increasingly apparent that all secondary schools need to provide students with appropriate career guidance and counseling to assist them in making informed decisions on a study path and occupational choices (Watts, 2013)—and many schools are now doing so. However, the quality and effectiveness of career counseling and guidance services vary widely across schools and systems (Loft et al., 2020; OECD, 2004; 2011).
It is vital that the personnel responsible for providing such support are well qualified and possess the appropriate expertise.

In Australia and the United States, rigorous career practitioner credentialing and licensure systems are already in place, but this is not necessarily the case in other locations.

One example is Hong Kong, where local authorities are only now working hard to raise the level of qualifications of general classroom teachers to perform career guidance and counseling work (Wong & Yuen, 2019) Aglobal survey, with more than 40,000 young people across 150 countries, found that 31% stated that the education they currently receive in school could not prepare them for the workplace (UNESCO, 2020; WorldSkills & OECD, 2019).

The same situation has been observed in Hong Kong (Shek et al., 2020). A study in 2019 surveyed more than 700 young people and their teachers from 103 secondary schools. Findings revealed that despite heavy government support in curriculum development and financial resources (in the form of a "Career and Life Planning Grant"), up to 30% of students opined that their schools still did little to encourage their career planning or expose them to various employment-related pathways and opportunities (Federation of Youth Groups, 2019; Wong & Yuen, 2019).

Relationship between teacher support and students' career development

During the adolescent stage, teachers play a major role in directly influencing the development of students' career aspirations, future orientation, career exploration, and planning (Alm et al., 2019; Hirschi et al., 2011; Rogers & Creed, 2011; Smylie & Smart, 1990). Empirical studies have found multiple therapeutic effects that teacher support can have on students' career planning and development.

These include development of positive career aspirations (Ali & McWhirter, 2006), career self-efficacy and outcome expectations (Gushue& Whitson, 2006), educational expectations (McWhirter et al., 1998) and school-related interest and goal orientations (Wentzel, 1998). Later benefits include readiness for career adaptability (Atac et al., 2018; Kenny & Bledsoe, 2005) and students anticipating fewer educational barriers or career barriers (Ali & McWhirter, 2006; McWhirter et al., 1998) and less attachment anxiety and distress (Luzzo et al., 1999; Vogel & Wei, 2005). In short, a major beneficial effect of CRTS is that it enhances students' positive schooling experience and maximizes their engagement in learning, which in turn enhances options for career planning (Lapan, 2004). Given the importance of teachers' career-related support (CRTS), a targeted review of this domain would be of benefit to improve career guidance and counseling practices at both group and

Factors that Affect Career Development

As identified by the theories of career choice highlighted above, one major variable that affects how people choose their occupations is personality traits. Holland (1987) argued that the choice of an occupation is an expression of personality and members of an occupation share similar personality characteristics.

Career interest is a second factor that affects the choice of a career. An interest may be conceived in terms of an activity which an individual engages in for the interest of it without deserving for an external reward. The reward is in the performance of the activity the person does. Personality and interest are not the only criteria for choosing a career.

An individual's aptitude and intellectual abilities are equally of great importance. An aptitude is a potential for success in an area after undergoing some training but a layman may define aptitude as a flair for something. The context in which people live, their personal aptitudes, and educational attainment are other things that do influence people's career choice.

(Bandura Barbaranelli Caprara & Pastorelli 2001) Similarly, skills and values also affect peoples' choices. Values are thè guiding principles that are ordered in importance and serve as standards for judging and justifying actions (Schwartz, 1992). In addition, Osakinle and Adegoroye (2008) identified factors that influence adolescents' choice of career as: sex, location of choice maker, environment, school influence (peer and curriculum content), and religious affi! iati on, child rearing and family values. In thè opinion of Morris and Levinson (1995); Pierce, McDermott, & Butkus, (2003), although intelligence is associated with career maturity and the development of decision making skills, factors other than skills, abilities, and personality play a major role in career development and satisfaction for people with mental retardation.

Factors such as interests, social opportunities, emotional rewards, and economie benefits influence career choices (of most adolescents, including those with cognitive limitations) (Szymanski, Hershenson, Enright, & Ettinger, 1996). In addition, Krumboltz, Mitchell and Jones (1976) opined that there are four factors that affect career choice of individuals. These are: genetic endowment and special abilities (such

Individual and Group Counselling

This is an important Service rendered to all students by guidance counsellors. Regular meetings with the guidance counsellor for either individual students or groups of students with special needs can be integrated into the IEP process to address educational and counselling needs, including career development plans and activities.

The American School Counsellor Association National Model (ASCA, 2003) provides a framework for guidance counsellors to help all students to "develop career awareness," "develop employment readiness," "acquire career information," "identify career" goals," "acquire knowledge to achieve career goals," and "apply skills to achieve career goals" (Campbell & Dahir

Career development activities within the educational setting may be the best opportunity for a student with special need to explore the world of work before entering private or state- federal vocational rehabilitation Service programmes for adults that focus primarily on job placement and tenure.

Individualized career development curricula can help document that students with special needs and their parents, educators, and advocates have information from which to make meaningful choices about the activities and outcomes of the IEP. The counsellor can teach decision-making skills. Guided decision-making exercises and planned opportunities for students to make important decisions and experience consequences in a safe environment are frequent used methods of teaching decision-making skills.

The guidance counsellor may have to apply different strategies with different categories of students with special needs when delivering career guidance to these students. For instance, thè future career paths of many students with mental retardation are likely to reflect a succession of employed positions at different settings rather than a single, sustained placement, because employment and job tenure continue to be low for adults with mental retardation (Pierce, McDermott, & Butkus, 2003; Schaffer, Banks, & Kregel, 1991). Therefore, thè guidance counsellor may expose young persons with mental retardation to several school-based leaming opportunities aimed at equipping them with useful vocational skills. These activities are particularly important for people with cognitive developmental disabilities who, unlike their peers without cognitive disabilities, may have limited opportunities to participate in social, work, volunteer, and community activities; and thus may have limited exposure to occupational role models.

For example, a vocational skill set that will transfer to multiple employment opportunities in clerical and reception occupations may include social skills (for example, appropriate socialization with peers and customers), mechanical skills (for example, the use of office equipment), safety skills (for example, seeking assistance), communication skills (for example, telephone etiquette), and hygiene skills (for example, appropriate dress and professional appearance).

Individuate with mental retardation often have difficulties generalizing work Behavior to new work settings; thus, the opportunity to practice skills across employment contexts is an essential part of developing a career that is resilient to changes in the labour market (Szymanski, 1999).

Further, for students with learning disabilities or for those who are academically gifted and talented, counsellors can encourage these students' teachers and parents to emphasize student abilities and talents, as opposed to focusing solely on their deficits. They can ateo encourage thè acquisition and use of compensation strategies to address leaming disabilities, such as books on tape and other technological aids, as well as the acquisition of targeted study and learning strategies (Reis, McGuire, & Neu, 2000). These materiate can centre on career awareness, vocational interests predominanti associated with their career choices, educational requirements of careers they desired and other career related issues. Abilities, interests, and talents can be assessed and counsellors can encourage the use of sometime both in school and at home that focuses on the development of students' talents and strengths. When educators view the successimi development of talents in these students with optimism and hope, more opportunities for school success may occur.

Educators and counsellor's ateo can help students to learn higher-order problem solving and information processing skills. As students' academic performances improve, students' self-confidence will increase and this will in tum enable the students to understand that they can perform assigned duties at work and they will readily pursue their desired careers with ease. Counsellor's ateo can help to encourage,

2.2 THE REASON AND OUTCOMES OF CAREER COUNSELLING

The career counselling process is a verbal procedure where a prepared vocation guide and customer are in a shared relationship, concentrated on using on the customers qualities and assets to settle on significant vocation related choices and oversee vocation related issues (Coetzee and Roythrone-Jacobs, 2012).The advocate utilizes an assortment of differing strategies and methods to enable the customer to settle on an educated choice on vocation decision

This choice must be made once the customer has arrived at a point of Self-understanding and understanding the vocation concerns required just as social alternatives accessible (Maree, 2004). Vocation directing arrangements with issues including the customers work, profession, life and jobs. The inquiries customers look for help for respect how clits see the present social, word related desires and open doors for vocation decision. Profession advocates help customers in breaking down desires and openings and guide customers to make a move and facilitate the tension and hesitance related with individual work life experiences(Coetzee and Roythrone-Jacobs,2012).Career instructors ought to furnish an individual with the capacity to comprehend and clarify the what, why, how their general life and vocation improvement assignments, challenges and the profession objectives they may have or the issues they may confront is significant particularly in a perplexing society and muddled workplace(Coetzee and Roythrone-Jacobs,2012).

People build up a feeling of character and significance through their vocations, in this way advocates should see customers in an extensive way by moving toward profession and way of life arranging in an individual and formative manner.

A viable vocation directing procedure encourages individuals to (Coetzee and Roythrone-Jacobs, 2012): Discover their enthusiasm recognize ones life reason and to manufacture a course of action forever ' Understand how to apply ones interesting abilities, gifts, values internal assets and beneficial experience to accomplish objectives Identify and change demoralizing convictions about themselves as well as other people Add an incentive to the working environment and individual they communicate with Strengthen esteemed

Connections by figuring out how to manage their own and others feelings by taking a gander at things in an alternate point of view ' Remove the hindrances to their very own imagination and development and grasp new difficulties and openings ' Resolve profession emergency just as to assume responsibility for their own vocation improvement Deal with things in a genuinely astute manner, for example, life occasions and advances.

Work life offset and manages potential stressors and strife circumstances in a genuinely innovative. The goal of the vocation guiding procedure is to improve the profession development and profession self-ability of customers with the goal that they are confident in settling on a decision that will bring satisfaction. This requires the

Vocation guide encourage profession development, profession flexibility, and vocation versatility as critical profession mental assets (Maree, 2004). The instructor will be required to direct the customer to build up their enthusiastic knowledge to advance self-assurance, profession versatility, vocation flexibility and a feeling of self-adequacy in taking care of profession changes, breaks, joblessness or underemployment. Vocation directing results likewise incorporate relearning and new adapting, just customers may need to unlearn messages about their capacity to accomplish in a specific field or their basic leadership capacities (Coetzee and RoythroneJacobs, 2012). They should relearn who they truly are , before they bargain of life and limit their vocation way they may for instance, need to relearn their affection for science.

They numerous additionally relearn old exercises, for example, they are answerable for their own satisfaction in any event, when others attempt to settle on choices for them

2.3 THE CAREER CHOICE THEORY BY JOHN HOLLAND

Holland's hypothesis depicts how people converge with their condition and how individual and ecological attributes bring about profession decisions and modification. The hypothesis manages specific character types and ecological models and investigates the association and fit among individual and condition (Stead and Watson, 2006). In this sense the hypothesis makes it conceivable to clarify the connection between the earth and character and the conduct that rises because of this collaboration.

People are attracted to a particular character job request of a word related condition that meets their own requirement for utilizing their aptitudes and capacities and communicating their frames of mind and qualities which will give them satisfaction (Coetzee and Roythrone-Jacobs 2007).

Holland makes reference to that by late adolescences individuals will look like a blend of professional character/premium sorts .The character types are R Realistic sort Investigative sort I Artistic sort A Social kind S Enterprising sort E Conventional sort C.
 Holland s six character types and six condition types exist parallel to one another framing a hexagon mirroring the qualities of the separate person. In this way, for instance the Artistic sorts have a closes association with the Social kind.

The hypothesis expresses that the vast majority look like multiple and now and again every one of the sorts in some degree.

A person's character is an interesting blend of the all the various kinds Coetzee and Roythrone-Jacobs (2007). The closer and people takes after a particular sort the more they show the qualities and practices of that type.

The sorts reliably show trademark scopes of conduct, examples of different preferences, explicit qualities and specific self-depictions. Profession and word related situations can be portrayed by the similarity and backing of the six character types.

Holland's hypothesis shows four builds which are useful in vocation guiding procedure: Congruence alludes to the reporters between a character type and the earth
The more comparable the character type is to the condition the more compatible the relationship.

People react better to situations which coordinate with their characters these conditions furnish them with circumstances and best satisfy their needs. For instance, a creative sort would fit better in a masterful domain. High congruency may prompt high employment fulfilment Stead and Watson (2006. Differentiation a few people or situations demonstrate more prominent similarity to a solitary sort for instance just imaginative is separated.

An individual or condition that shows various sorts of a similar degree for instance, one is pretty much similarly masterful , analytical and venturesome is undifferentiated ' Consistency alludes to how much a few sorts and conditions share more practically speaking than different kinds and condition. Types on inverse corners of the hexagon are alternate extremes while those neighbours are comparable. For instance, the practical, analytical sorts share more for all intents and purpose with the than the reasonable social sorts.

Identity alludes to how much an individual has a reasonable stable present and future image of their objectives. The Holland framework is a well know model should an advisor consider utilizing this framework they ought to consider the accompanying : ' Holland's hypothesis isn't intended for analyst the hypothesis can be applied by educator's faculty labourer HR troughs and profession show coordinators

The hypothesis isn't limited to one on one directing in particular. Holland's notices that vocation right hand activities can be in a more extensive setting. Holland's hypothesis is valuable to customers since it consolidates word related data into the guiding procedure by giving a hypothetical edge work of potential occupations for customers.

2.4 THE CAREER DEVELOPMENT THEORY OF DONALD SUPER

Supers hypothesis is related with the formative way to deal with vocations. Super accepted that a person's vocation decision is simply the aftereffect of his/her idea. One's self idea can be portrayed as ones perspective on their very own attributes for instance their ones capacities, qualities, interests, and decisions. Self-idea creates through a person's collaboration with the earth, wherein the individual creates ideas of themselves in specific jobs, for example, an understudy, labourer, companion or relative.

How much an individual feel they can apply his/hers self-idea through their work decisions, impacts the degree of fulfilment in a particular word related condition (Coetzee and Roy throne-Jacobs 2007). One of Supers major centres is the idea of life jobs and speaks to the acknowledgment that work job may not be the fundamental job in a person's life space. The work job should be comprehended as far as the setting of all the existence jobs of and person. Pretending starts at youth when jobs, for example, nurture ,sales rep and instructor are carried on and it proceeds in adulthood when people envision themselves in the job for instance of a CEO, director. Pretending is utilitarian whether it is in dream or reality, or in a work or non-business related circumstance it will add to profession alteration.

The significance of any life job will depend upon the person's life arrange (Coetzee and Roy throne-Jacobs 2007). An individual will experience a progression of life stages called smaller than expected cycles and maxi cycle, each requiring the achievement of various profession formative errands. The vocation related stages are alluded to as smaller than usual cycles while the grown-up life stages are alluded to as the maxi cycle's .Career change is identified with profession development which incorporates practices that are good to alteration. Vocation development isn't age related however gauges the preparation to settle on profession choices and to adapt to the formative undertakings of unmistakable life stages.

The achievement of a progress between the five life stages relies upon the person's vocation development. Vocation development is the basic leadership capacity; profession arranging and comprehension of the universe of work .A profession advocate can survey a person's profession development by assessing the person's basic leadership aptitudes, arranging capacity, sensible self-examination, customer's information on formative undertakings and occupations.

As grown-ups move in to the foundation period of their lives and professions they need a significant level of vocation development and a need to create profession versatility to keep being utilized in the changing universe of work (Coetzee and Roy throne-Jacobs 2007). This hypothesis can be helpful to vocation advocates in thinking about age related issues being significant to customers. Vocation advocates ought to likewise take note of how a people esteems have changed during the existence stages

2.5 Inspecting factors which impact career improvement

`The second point that helps your career movement is the attention on elements affecting your present profession improvement. The counsellor will assist students with recognizing the various issues that can affect students career movement these are includes

2.5.1 Individual factors–

If you have a family to help, profession advocate will help recognize career objectives with you, which line up with your family's needs. For example, in the event that you can't stand to quit working while at the same time evolving professions, the advisor can help distinguish appr

2.5.2 Worth based factors–

These incorporate things you need from your activity, yet in addition explicit esteems that may impact your activity fulfilment. For instance, you should discover a job that spotlights on social equity.

2.5.3 Instructive factors –

What are the aptitudes you have and how might you keep on studyinoaches acquiring abilities while working Instructive factors – What are the aptitudes you have and how might you keep on studying your picked industry? Profession guide will assist map with excursion the instructive scene, both as far as the past and what's to come

2.5.4 Capacity based elements –

You'll likewise look at the capacity-based things affecting your profession movement. This is a mix of analysing your experience and finding various approaches to expand the experience. For instance, temporary positions may be an appropriate choice for you or you ought to think about seeking after your new profession as a side interest first

Seeing how every one of the above variables is affecting your profession movement, both as far as impeding it or boosting it, you can centre your endeavours in procedures that work the best. For example, you may see your instruction is hindering your picked career movement and keeping you from advancements. With the assistance of a lifelong instructor, you can begin investigating approaches to teach and prepare yourself further.

2.6 D-R gravy of Wixom assistant commissioner Utah system of higher education October 12-2016.

This is right that students have little information about the word career counselling. So, this is notified with the help of different research that a professional career counsellor is hopefully needs to enable students on the best path or rather counsel them on the field of interest. Career counselling play a key role to open the doors for the self-exploration of students and it also enable the personal skills of students in educational career. Unlike self-counselling and career counselling are two interrelated fields of study which build up strong and productive future of students. Psychological motivation is totally different from career counselling. As career counselling had enough influence on character building while psychology is more concern with the student's mental response. Impact of career counselling is the right way to assemble the whole natural capabilities of students

If a student had gone through the process of career counselling, he may not face any difficulty at different stages of life. The word career counselling is absolutely clear with the different sources that ensure a pivotal presence to motivate a student for career counselling. For instance source I-e. Social media TV book and etc. students can acknowledge various ways of career guidance and then they go to understand the basic positive impact of it. (Career counselling a holistic approach by Vernon G Zunker

2.7 Career counselling in Islamabad.

Career counselling is prestigious as career assistance, counselling and examined configuration to encourage with picking, moving, or leaving a career and may be gotten to at any phase throughout everyday life. One's career is as often as possible one of the most basic highlights of the prime of life, and carry on another profession, regardless of whether for the underlying time, the moment time, or whenever a short time later, can be a difficult occasion, particularly when financial troubles, for example, gloom are a development.

A career counsellor can help out by division and talking about one's forthcoming profession decisions by showing them the correct way conveying forward to an effective profession way. The instructive crisis guarantees announced by the legislature and some global nonrevenue driven associations taking a shot at instructive area are being uncovered in Baluchistan region as it has been watched, there is no any career counselling held for the individuals of Islamabad for a long time.

The numbers show the non-reality of higher specialists and their protections in this regard, which isn't sufficient to kill the sentiment of destitution of the individuals of Baluchistan. It is a significant occasion to be discussed in light of the fact that few hundred students from Islamabad whose degrees and degree decisions don't meet.

They end up doing a task that is unseemly to their long periods of instruction, causing in an absence of productivity and minor continues. This doesn't just hinder association's advancement yet additionally has horrendous outcomes in an individual's life coordinating to wretchedness and occupation endures weariness.

To contradict this event, mankind is employing the administrations of profession advisors. Counselling is a mystery and joint procedure where a career counsellor helps students in their instructive and career the executives. Fortunately, it's anything but an obscure articulation for us yet the choices and strategies are pending in this issue causing vulnerability and uneasy.

The proposals holding up under the suggestion of higher specialists and the mindful characters of the state would figure out how to contract career counsellors in each accessible college and school to organize career counselling classes, workshops and preparing bring mindfulness among the populace of any age particularly youth to pick a more secure profession way for their confident future. This will carry the people groups' enthusiasm to put their significant offer in the improvement of society as they are among the recipients.

It may empower them to acquire a history for themselves as well as for their nation. It will flaunt their certainty to tolerate out a superior life and pass on them over the span of dynamic individuals whose craving to do well for their nation's notoriety and development. Being steadfast with our educational segment as a social activist, It is my prime obligation to pass on the upsides and downsides of career counselling ahead to lead my more youthful age towards quality educating and a commitment, giving the quality protection of career way by reconciling the benevolent consideration of concern specialists to embrace a harder notice against the issue and get some helpful methodology by executing career counselling in government level

2.7.1. STUDENT VOICE LINKED TO CAREERS EDUCATION AND GUIDANCE

The writing on understudy voice likewise connections to vocations instruction and direction where it is proposed understudies ought to be counselled so as to adopt an all-encompassing strategy, as every understudy has an alternate arrangement of impacts which influence basic leadership and a constructivist approach is bound to influence purchase in from the understudies.

Vaughan (2003) states that immaturity is a crucial time of self-disclosure and future arranging, so counselling understudies on how professions instruction and direction could be conveyed What's more, what is essential to understudies may upgrade both acknowledgment of, and activity on, the guidance given via vocation instructors. This is additionally alluded to as „constructivist learning" which expects understudies to play a progressively dynamic job in the development of their learning (Levin, 2000). Levin (2000) declares that "students" work in schools can't be isolated from the progressions occurring in their lives outside of school; that changes in apparent work openings or family structures or sexual orientation jobs impact sly affect how understudies see and react to what the school gives" (p. 158).

People don't live in segregation and their social framework, in addition to cultural framework, impact vocation advancement and decisions (Patton and McMahon, 2006). Vaughan (2003) notes generally little research has been done where youthful people's encounters are put at the middle and she recommends that vocations training "examine and approach is organized by very specific ideas of youth, adulthood and change", (p. 1) which has been created by grown-ups. She additionally recommends it isn't so a lot of what pathways youthful individuals pick, or where they go to after school in a customary following examination venture that tally, but instead how they explore these pathways (Vaughan, 2003). Toda's accentuation on singular duty and decision mean youngsters are under expanding strain to settle on educated profession choices at a generally youthful age which can have sweeping ramifications for their fates. Access to pertinent professions instruction and to work in organization with guardians, instructors and Careers Advisors is along these lines basic to great basic leadership (Horne, 2010; Vaughan, 2003). Vaughan and Roberts (2007) declare a profession venture is an extremely intricate, nondirect pathway which takes numerous turns and turns over a person's lifetime and we have to all the more likely comprehend the job of "tumult or eccentrics in vocation choices and what devices may be valuable to assist individuals with overseeing it" (p. 103)

Patton also, McMahon (2006) propose that by counselling understudies we can all the more likely comprehend their individual circumstances, what influences their vocation basic leadership, and what professions instruction and support is applicable to guarantee deep rooted learning and achievement in a regularly changing and dynamic universe of work.

The importance of career counselling

In order to understand the development of career guidance and counseling in Hong Kong, it is important to appreciate how the work is generally perceived in relation to China's cultural traditions. Long before the emergence of recent concepts like guidance or counseling, the notion of striving for holistic educational and spiritual experiences had long existed in Chinese philosophy. This suggests that, in the Chinese mindset, guidance and counseling must be an integral part of a well-rounded education (Fong, 2001).

Defining support from teachers

The concept of 'general teacher support' has been studied under many different categorizations (e.g. classroom belonging, student guidance, individual counseling, pastoral care, pedagogical caring, relatedness). All these labels basically refer to the same notion that teacher support operates via 2 intellectual and emotional bonds that exist between students and teachers (Davis, 2003; Pringle et al. (L.P.W, 2020)

CHAPTER 3

3. Research Methodology

Population sample and sampling Methodology

The research included 200 students from government secondary schools in the Islamabad i.9.4 A total of 100 students were chosen for the analysis using a simple random sampling method.

Research design

The study of this research was qualitative in nature opting exploratory design and distributed research questionnaire in the Osama Bin Tariq shaheed model school for boys I/9.4 Islamabad

Validity

Validity simply means that a test or instrument is accurately measuring what it is supposed to measure. In this study, questionnaire was used to collect the data that is and its validity was determined through pilot testing and expert opinion.

Reliability

Reliability can be defined as the degree to which measurements are free from error and therefore give consistent results. In other words, reliability concerns the extent to which a test or any measuring procedure yields the same results on repeated trials. Reliability of instrument used in this study was determined through test-retest method.

Sample technique

This statement identifies that the sample technique is the procedure through which a researcher choose the way of specifying the respondents from the universe. Due to less time, finical problems and etc. the researcher could not study the whole universe in short period of time My sample technique is probability sample, where each individual have equal chance to participate in the study. Inside the probability sampling I have selected random sampling

Tools for data collection

This statement identifies those tools for data collection which a researcher collect data for his research study. There are different tools for data collection. And I for this research study tools of data collection questionnaire. The data has been collected through questionnaire form the respondents of sample size from the targeted universe

3.5. Questionnaire

Questionnaire is a series of questions, used to gather information from the respondents. The questions are used for audience analysis and they are meant to create an understanding of the targeted respondents form the selected universe. And the researcher wants to know the response, feelings, perceptions, and beliefs about the asked questions in a questionnaire paper.

1.5.1. Pilot testing

Pilot testing also called free testing; it is a process through which a researcher distributes few questionnaires to the non-respondents, before distributing original questionnaire to the respondents In which researcher removes all the invalid questions and difficulties from the questinnairs

CHAPTER 4

Data analysing

4.1.1. Table No 1

Have you ever heard the word career counselling?

Categories	Frequency	Percentage
Yes	76	76%
No	8	8%
To some extent	12	12%
No idea	04	4%
Respondent	100	100%

Table 01 show those 76% respondents agree with "yes"08% respondents agree with "no"12% respondent with "to some extend"04% respondents agree with "no idea: Total respondent are 100%

Table 4.1.2.

Do you agree that career counselling has enough concern with the student's future

Categories	Frequency	Percentage
Yes	54	54%
No	08	08%
To some extent	20	20%
No idea	18	18%

Respondent	100	100%

Table 02 show those 54% respondents agree with "yes"08% respondents agree with "no"20% respondent with "to some extend"18% respondent agrees with "no idea: Total respondent are 100%

Table No 4.1.3.

At which stage life educational life career counselling should be given to the student for bring future?

Categories	Frequency	Percentage
Yes	60	60%
No	26	26%
To some extent	08	08%
No idea	06	06%
Total Respondent	100	100%

Table 03 show those 60% respondents agree with "yes"26% respondents agree with "no"08% respondent with "to some extend"06% respondents agree with "no idea: Total respondent are 100%

Table No 4.1.4.

Do you are that career counselling enhance the ability and skills of student

Categories	Frequency	Percentage

Yes	52	52%
No	12	12%
To some extent	30	30%
No idea	06	06%
Respondent	100	100%

Table 04 show those 52% respondents agree with "yes"12% respondents agree with "no"30% respondent with "to some extend"06% respondents agree with "no idea: Total respondent are 100%

Table No 4.1.5.

Can career counselling upgrade the mental power of student?

Categories	Frequency	Percentage
Yes	52	52%
No	12	12%
To some extent	30	30%
No idea	06	06%
Respondent	100	100%

Table 05 show that 52%respondent agrees with "yes"12% respondents agrees with "no"30% respondent with "to some extend"06% respondent agrees with "no idea: Total respondent are 100%

Table No 4.1.6

Do you agree that career counselling is the best discipline for student to meet future goals?

Category	Frequency	Percentage
Yes	50	50%
No	10	10%
To some extent	20	20%
No idea	20	20%
Respondent	100	100%

Table 06 show that 50%respondent agrees with "yes"10% respondents agree with "no"20% respondent with "to some extend"20% respondent agree with "no idea: Total respondent are 100%

Table No 4.1.7.

Do you that career counselling influence students educational performance?

Category	Frequency	Percentage
Yes	50	50%
No	06	06%
To some extent	38	38%
No idea	06	06%
Respondent	100	100%

Table 07 show that 50%respondent agree with "yes"06% respondents agree with "no"38% respondent with "to some extend"06% respondent agree with "no idea: Total respondent are 100%

Table No 4.1.8.

Does student bright future depend on career counselling?

Category	Frequency	Percentage
Yes	32	32%
No	28	28%
To some extent	24	24%
No idea	16	16%
Respondent	100	100%

Table 08 shows that 32%respondent agrees with "yes"28% respondents agree with "no"24% respondents with "to some extend"16% respondent agree with "no idea: Total respondent are 100%

Table No 4.1.9.

Q No: 9 where you suggested to a counsellor while choosing current field of study?

Category	Frequency	Percentage
Yes	24	24%
No	58	58%
To some extent	06	06%

| No idea | 12 | 12% |
| Respondent | 100 | 100% |

Table 09 show that24%respondent agree with "yes"58% respondents agree with "no"06% respondent with "To Some Extend"12% respondent agree with "No Idea: Total respondent are 100%

TABLE NO 4.1.10.

Are you satisfied from your current field?

Category	Frequency	Percentage
Yes	54	54%
No	10	10%
To some extent	36	36%
No idea	0	0%
Respondent	100	100%

Table 10 show that54%respondent agree with "yes"10% respondents agree with "no"36% respondent with "to some extend"0% respondent agree with "no idea: Total respondent are 100%

Table No 4.1.11

What you do think you would have been chosen a batter field of study if were counselled by a professional counsellor?

Category	Frequency	Percentage
Yes	62	62%
No	18	18%
To some extent	12	12%
No idea	08	08%
Respondent	100	100%

Table 11 show that62%respondent agree with "yes"18% respondents agree with "no"12% respondent with "to some extend"08% respondent agree with "no idea: Total respondent are 100%

Table No

Table No 4.1.12.

Do you agree that career counselling makes student more competitive and conscious toward their future goals?

Category	Frequency	Percentage
Yes	56	56%
No	04	04%
To some extent	34	34%
No idea	06	06%
Respondent	100	100%

Table 12 show those 56% respondents agree with "yes"04% respondents agree with "no"34% respondent with "to some extend"06% respondents agree with "no idea: Total respondent are 100%

Table No 4.1.13

Does career counselling has positive impact on student's career building?

Category	Frequency	Percentage
Yes	62	62%
No	06	06%
To some extent	22	22%
No idea	10	10%
Respondent	100	100%

Table 13 show those 62% respondents agree with "yes"06% respondents agree with "no"22% respondent with "to some extend"10% respondents agree with "no idea: Total respondent are 100%

Table No 4.1.14.

Do you agree that career counselling enable student to deal with different issues in educational career?

Category	Frequency	Percentage
Yes	56	56%
No	08	08%
To some extent	28	28%

| No idea | 08 | 08% |
| Respondent | 100 | 100% |

Table 14 show those 56 % respondents agree with "yes"08% respondents agree with "no"28% respondent with "to some extend"08% respondents agree with "no idea: Total respondent are 100%

Table No 4.1.15.

Can career counselling provides a satisfactory occupation for student in future?

Category	Frequency	Percentage
Yes	30	30%
No	22	22%
To some extent	26	26%
No idea	22	22%
Respondent	100	100%

Table 15 show those 30 % respondents agree with "yes"22% respondents agree with "no"26% respondent with "to some extend"22% respondents agree with "no idea: Total respondent are 100%

Table No 4.1.16.

Q No 16 It is true that career counselling gave a second pair of eyes to student to go through their abilities?

Category	Frequency	Percentage

Category	Frequency	Percentage
Yes	42	42%
No	10	10%
To some extent	32	32%
No idea	16	16%
Respondent	100	100%

Table 16 show those 42 % respondents agree with "yes"10% respondents agree with "no"32% respondent with "to some extend"16% respondents agree with "no idea: Total respondent are 100%

Table No 4.1.17.

Who is the responsible for lack of career counselling?

Category	Frequency	Percentage
Yes	46	30%
No	18	22%
To some extent	20	26%
No idea	16	16%
Respondent	100	100%

Table 17 show those 46 % respondents agree with "yes"18% respondents agree with "no"20% respondent with "to some extend"16% respondents agree with "no idea: Total respondent are 100%

TABLE NO 4.1.18.

Should we rise for proper career counselling facilities in secondary schools level ?

Category	Frequency	Percentage
Yes	92	92%
No	04	04%
To some extent	02	02%
No idea	02	02%
Respondent	100	100%

Table 18 show that 92 %respondent agrees with "yes"04% respondents agrees with "no"02% respondent with "to some extend"02% respondent agree with "no idea: Total respondent are 100%

Table No 4.1.19.

19 Do you have resources to accomplish the aim of life?

Category	Frequency	Percentage
Yes	26	26%
No	34	44%
To some extent	40	42%
No idea	12	12%
Respondent	100	100%

Table 19 show that 26 %respondent agree with "yes"34% respondents agree with "no"04% respondent with "to some extend"12% respondent agree with "no idea: Total respondent are 100%

Table No 4.1.20

Itself interest being the main source in achievement of educational career goals?

Category	Frequency	Percentage
Yes	50	50%
No	12	12%
To some extent	24	24%
No idea	14	14%
Respondent	100	100%

Table 20 show that 50 %respondent agree with "yes"12% respondents agree with "no"24% respondent with "to some extend"14% respondent agree with "no idea: Total respondent are 100%

4.2.Results and findings

Under this statement (To analysis the impacts of career counselling on student's educational performance) of the research study is a qualitative research and the information was assembled through questionnaire form the respondents. In that process the researcher has asked different questions from the respondents about the impacts of career counselling on students' educational performance. All the selected respondents have responded very well and attractive. As they responded, the following are the findings and results of whole questionnaire. Majority of the respondents were aware about the statement of career counselling.

And they were having enough concern to the career counselling. Majority of the respondents have agreed that career counselling has more concern towards student's future. Half of the respondents have considered school to be the first stage of career counselling, and it should be provided at school level, which brings more efficiency of condense and interest in a student for his study, that can lead him towards success.

Career counselling has more concern to enhance the student's inner abilities and skills which motivate them to work professionally and technically. Which really give great anthurium to students to concentrate for improvement their mental capabilities? Half of the respondents had considered that career counselling is the best discipline in future to meet their goals.

In this study it was more focused that career counselling influences the educational performance of students at any level of life. The success of students depends on career counselling. It provides the best way to go through their future goals. Majority of the respondents have agreed and mentioned that the failure of many students in their educational career is due to the lack of career counselling process.

Every institution should provide the best career counselling sessions for students to decrease the failure ratio of students. 85% of the respondents have responded that we have never suggested to a professional counsellor, that he can guide us properly about self-interested subject. When students are prepared to counsellors so dignity they will face difficulties in their field of study

When students are consoled by a counsellor so they would choose the best field of study to achieve future goals Career counselling makes students more competitive and conscious about their studies, and the jelsy factor reflects them to work hard with full concentration. Career counselling has positive impacts which build the productive career of a student. Many of the respondents have responded that parents are more responsible for the lack of career counselling, because parents are the primary agents of socialization process and they can understand the psycho of their children's that in which field of study their Childers's are interest and what they are capable to do in future.

Findings

The role of teachers in career counselling at secondary level in Islamabad

1. Table 01 show those 76% respondents agree with "yes"08% respondents agree with "no"12% respondent with "to some extend"04% respondents agree with "no idea: Total respondent are 100%

2. Table 02 show those 54% respondents agree with "yes"08% respondents agree with "no"20% respondent with "to some extend"18% respondent agrees with "no idea: Total respondent are 100%

3. Table 03 show those 60% respondents agree with "yes"26% respondents agree with "no"08% respondent with "to some extend"06% respondents agree with "no idea: Total respondent are 100%

4. Table 04 show those 52% respondents agree with "yes"12% respondents agree with "no"30% respondent with "to some extend"06% respondents agree with "no idea: Total respondent are 100%

5. Table 05 show that 52%respondent agrees with "yes"12% respondents agrees with "no"30% respondent with "to some extend"06% respondent agrees with "no idea: Total respondent are 100%

6. Table 06 show that 50%respondent agrees with "yes"10% respondents agree with "no"20% respondent with "to some extend"20% respondent agree with "no idea: Total respondent are 100%

7. Table 07 show that 50%respondent agree with "yes"06% respondents agree with "no"38% respondent with "to some extend"06% respondent agree with "no idea: Total respondent are 100%

8. Table 08 shows that 32%respondent agrees with "yes"28% respondents agree with "no"24% respondents with "to some extend"16% respondent agree with "no idea: Total respondent are 100%

9. Table 09 show that24%respondent agree with "yes"58% respondents agree with "no"06% respondent with "To Some Extend"12% respondent agree with "No Idea: Total respondent are 100%

10. Table 10 show that54%respondent agree with "yes"10% respondents agree with "no"36% respondent with "to some extend"0% respondent agree with "no idea: Total respondent are 100%

11. Table 11 show that62%respondent agree with "yes"18% respondents agree with "no"12% respondent with "to some extend"08% respondent agree with "no idea: Total respondent are 100%

12. Table 12 show those 56% respondents agree with "yes"04% respondents agree with "no"34% respondent with "to some extend"06% respondents agree with "no idea: Total respondent are 100%

13. Table 13 show those 62% respondents agree with "yes"06% respondents agree with "no"22% respondent with "to some extend"10% respondents agree with "no idea: Total respondent are 100%

14. Table 14 show those 56 % respondents agree with "yes"08% respondents agree with "no"28% respondent with "to some extend"08% respondents agree with "no idea: Total respondent are 100%

15. Table 15 show those 30 % respondents agree with "yes"22% respondents agree with "no"26% respondent with "to some extend"22% respondents agree with "no idea: Total respondent are 100%

16. Table 16 show those 42 % respondents agree with "yes"10% respondents agree with "no"32% respondent with "to some extend"16% respondents agree with "no idea: Total respondent are 100%

17. Table 17 show those 46 % respondents agree with "yes"18% respondents agree with "no"20% respondent with "to some extend"16% respondents agree with "no idea: Total respondent are 100%

18. Table 18 show that 92 %respondent agrees with "yes"04% respondents agrees with "no"02% respondent with "to some extend"02% respondent agree with "no idea: Total respondent are 100%

19. Table 19 show that 26 %respondent agree with "yes"34% respondents agree with "no"04% respondent with "to some extend"12% respondent agree with "no idea: Total respondent are 100%

20. Table 20 show that 50 %respondent agree with "yes"12% respondents agree with "no"24% respondent with "to some extend"14% respondent agree with "no idea: Total respondent are 100%

CHAPTER No 5

Discussion and Conclusion

The whole crux of this research study is that career counselling has tremendous impacts on student's educational performance at university of IIUI But unfortunately, university is failed to provide proper facilities of career counselling. More than enough students of Islamabad province are choosing their careers without gaining their personal goals and field of interest. 60% of the students were unaware about the term of career counselling, and that cause majority of the student's failed in their field of study.

Students are not receiving any career counselling at any level in the academic life Most of the respondent were more conscious for the proper facilities of career counselling at provincial level. However, students consider that career counselling play a crucial role in the progress and development of student's educational performance.

A student needs career counselling disparately for their bright future and their field of interest. In this study it has founded that more students were not guided or counselled to choose their field of study. Punjab province isn't have a valid or formal system of career counselling, and that is worse for the students of Islamabad as they usually failed to go through in their educational career.

So, there must be the negative effects of student's failure of future goals. If govt doesn't provide career counselling facilities to the students at any level of educational intuitions Furthered more in this research study, I have founded that all the students of Islamabad secondary level schools students were not convinced by the university management to provide proper career counselling facilities. More than 80% of the respondents were not suggested to professional career counsellors to choose their current field of study or field of interest.

Most of the students blindly follow their siblings, friends and parents for their educational careers and that become the cause of failed of their educational careers. Most of the students were not satisfied from their current field of study and they were facing difficulties in current field of study. However, 62% of the student's responded that if school or college provide career counselling to the student' at basic level of education, so, they would have chosen a batter field of study to achieve future goals and destiny.

Career counsellor must be a professional person in counselling who have knowledge about student's psychology and more who is capable to measure and identify the personality of a student. It was founded that career counselling can play significant role in the valid selection of educational careers. So moreover,

It is very essential for Punjab province to establish a separate department for career counselling at all level of educational intuitions in a positive sense to make students to choose what they love to do in their future.

If the best and formal selection is done through proper career counselling, majority of the can contribute in the development and progress of the society.

5.1. Suggestions and Recommendations

Statement of this study is about to analysis the impacts of career counselling on student educational performance. So, I have decided to recommend some major recommendations for the future study.

• This topic should bring under extensive research to more accurately to find the impacts of career counselling on students' performance.

• Media has an important role to play while highlighting the importance and benefits of career counselling

. • During instructing subject instructor may educate understudies about attributes and extent of different occupations.

• University may sort out courses/workshops/to give understudies data about different occupations, and capability required for explicit calling, extent of different callings, and their future advantages. Thusly understudies may be educated/up dated about applicable employment data

• Different ventures might be welcome in colleges to oversee work reasonable at colleges and along these lines' understudies might be make up dated about different kinds of callings and their necessities.

• College training level is the most significant level in understudies' life; along these lines, at the hour of confirmation, the college may give a flyers or hand-outs that may give complete data about the future limit/points of interest of the courses.

• Further looks into on vocation guiding needs of optional what's more, higher optional in light of the fact that understudies need to take major choices about determination of subjects at higher auxiliary level.

• Further investigations may be carried out to explore the effects of career counselling on performance of students and effects of career counselling may be explored on employees' job satisfaction.

References

*Ali, S. R., & McWhirter, E. H. (2006). Rural Appalachian youth's vocational/educational

Adolescence,34(1)163 172. https://doi.org/10.1016/j.adolescence.2009.12.010.

Bandura, A Barbaranelli, C., Caprara, G. V., & Pastorelli, C. (2001). Self-efficacy beliefs as

shapers of children' aspirations and career trajectories Child Development 72, 187-206.

Counseling Psychology 53(3) 379–385. https://doi.org/10.1037/0022-0167.53.3.379

Career Development, 102(1), 81-94.

(L.P.W, 2020)

Culver, S., Welfare, L., & Sanders, C. (2017). Career Counseling in Middle Schools: A

Study of School Counselor Self-Efficacy. The Professional Counselor, 239.

Dondo, M.(2006).Guidance and counselling for Schools and Colleges. Nairobi: Christian

Education Association Press

Denga, H.(2004).The influence of gender on occupational aspirations of primary school

children in Cross River State. The African Symposium, 4(2), 26-31.

Elizabeth, M. A. (2012).Factors Affecting Career Aspirations of Girls; Emerging Issues and

Challenges (Unpublished Master Theses), Department of Education, Kenyatta University

Fong, L. (2001, 4 April 1). The improtance. *Career guidance and Counselling in sendary

school in Hong Kong, 9*(2019). Onttrek may monday, 2001

Foskett et al., (2008).The influence of the school in the decision to participate in learning post

16. British Educational Research Journal, 34(1), 37-61.

Garrahy, D.A.(2001).Three third grade teachers' genders beliefs and behaviors. Journal of

Gushue, G. V. & Whitson, M. L. (2006) The relationship of ethnic identity and gender role attitudes to the development of career choice goals among black and Latina girls Journal of Howard,et, al. (2009).The relation of cultural context and social relationships to career development in middle schools. Journal of Vocational Behavior, 75, 100-108.

* Hirschi, A. (2012). The career resources model: an integrative framework for career

Khan, H.Murtaza, F., & Shifa, M. D.(2012). The Role of Teachers in Providing Educational and Career Guidance To The Secondary School Students in Gilgit Baltistan, Pakistan. International Journal of Academic Research 1 (2), 85-102.

. Kisilu,J., Kimani, E., & Kombo, D. (2012). Factors influencing occupational aspirations among girls in secondary schools in Nairobi, kenya. Prime Journal, 2 (4), 244-251

* Kenny, M. E., & Bledsoe, M. (2005). Contributions of the relational context to career adaptability among urban adolescents. Journal of Vocational Behavior, 66(2), 257–272. https://doi.org/10.1016/j.jvb.2004.10.002

.Luzzo, D. A., Hasper, P., Albert, K. A., Bibby, M. A., & Martinelli, E. A. J. (1999). Effects of self-efficacy -enhancing interventions on the math/science self-efficacy and career interests, goals, and actions of career undecided college students. Journal of Counseling Psychology 46(2), 233–243 https://doi.org/10.1037/0022-0167.46.2.233

M. Szymanski & R. P. Parker (Eds.), Work and disability: Issues and strategies in career development and job placement (pp. 80-117). Austin, TX: PRO-ED.

Morris, T.W & Levinson E. M. (1995) Relationship between intelligence and occupational adjustment and functioning: A literature review. Journal of Counseling and Development 73,503-514

* McWhirter, E. H., Hackett, G., & Bandalos D. L. (1998). A causal model of the educational plans and career expectations of Mexican American high school girls Journal of Counseling Psychology 45(2), 166–181 https://doi.org/10.1037/0022-0167.45.2.16

M. Szymanski & R. P. Parker (Eds.), Work and disability: Issues and strategies in career development and job placement (pp. 80-117). Austin, TX: PRO-ED.

Rogers, M. E.& Creed, P. A. (2011).A longitudinal examination of adolescent career x

Szymanski, E. M., Hershenson, D. B., Enright, M. S., & Ettinger, J. M. (1996). Career

Shek, D.T.L., Lin, L., Ma, C.M.S., Yu, L., Leung, J.T.Y., Wu, F.K.Y., Leung, H., & Dou, D. (2020) Perceptions of adolescents, teachers and parents of life skills education and life skills in high school students in Hong Kong. Applied Research in Quality of Life https://doi.org/10.1007/s11482-020 09848-9

Shumba,A., & Naong, M. (2012).Factors Influencing Students Career Choices and Aspirations in South Africa. Journal of Social Sciences 33 (2), 169-178.

Szymanski, E. M. (1999). Disability, job stress, the changing nature of careers, and thè career resilience portfolio Rehabilitation Counseling Bulletin, 42, 279-289.

WATSON, M. M. (2009, july, september friday). National education policy. *Dr. Alam Zeb, 1*(2,2021)

Watts, A.G. (2013). Career guidance and orientation

Watson, M.,mcmahon, M., Foxcroft, C., & Els, C.(2010).Occupational aspirations of low socio-economic African children. *Journal of Career Development, 37*(4), 17-34.

Appendix-A

QUESTIONNER FOR TEACHERS

Dear Teacher

, I am students of BS Education at International Islamic University Islamabad. My research topic is The Role of teachers in career counselling at Secondary School Level in Islamabad". I am collecting data. In this regard, one questionnaire is dispatched. Can you please spare 20 minutes to fill it out? I shall be thankful for your cooperation.

Yours truly

Nawaz Sharif

BS Scholar

IIUI

Name   (Optional): _________________   Name   of   School: _______________   Gender: ___________ please read the statements carefully and tick (√) the most appropriate option. YES = NO = TO SOME EXTEND= NO IDEA :

Statement					
Role of teachers in career guidance at secondary school level in Islamabad					
Have you ever heard the word career counselling?					
Do you agree that career counselling has enough concern with the student's future?					
At which stage life educational life career counselling should be given to the student for bring future?					
Do you are that career counselling enhance the ability and skills of student?					

Question					
Can career counselling upgrade the mental power of student?					
Do you agree that career counselling is the best discipline for student to meet future goals?					
Do you that career counselling influence students educational performance?					
Does student bright future depend on career counselling?					
Where you suggested to a counsellor while choosing current field of study?					
Are you satisfied from your current field?					
What you do think you would have been chosen a batter field of study if were counselled by a professional counsellor?					
Do you agree that career counselling makes student more competitive and conscious toward their future goals?					
Does career counselling have positive impact on student's career building?					
Do you agree that career counselling enable student to deal with different issues in educational career?					
Can career counselling provide a satisfactory occupation for student in future?					

yes

I want morebooks!

Buy your books fast and straightforward online - at one of world's fastest growing online book stores! Environmentally sound due to Print-on-Demand technologies.

Buy your books online at
www.morebooks.shop

Kaufen Sie Ihre Bücher schnell und unkompliziert online – auf einer der am schnellsten wachsenden Buchhandelsplattformen weltweit! Dank Print-On-Demand umwelt- und ressourcenschonend produzi ert.

Bücher schneller online kaufen
www.morebooks.shop

Printed by Books on Demand GmbH, Norderstedt / Germany